TRAILBLAZERS OF THE WEST

THE GOLD RUSH
Buried Treasure

★ ★ ★

Barbara A. Somervill

HIGH
interest
books

Children's Press®
A Division of Scholastic Inc.
New York / Toronto / London / Auckland / Sydney
Mexico City / New Delhi / Hong Kong
Danbury, Connecticut

Book Design: Mindy Liu and Erica Clendening
Contributing Editors: Matt Pitt and Kevin Somers
Photo Credits: Cover, pp. 17, 24, 26, 36 © Bettmann/Corbis; p. 4 © Steve
Starr/Corbis; pp. 7, 8, 34 © Corbis; p. 11 Courtesy of the Bancroft Library,
University of California, Berkeley; p. 18 © Ron Watts/Corbis; p. 21 © Museum
of the City of New York/Corbis; pp. 22–23 © L. Clarke/Corbis; p. 29 © Topham/The
Image Works; p. 30 © Joseph Sohm/The Image Works; p. 33 © Getty Images;
p. 38 Library of Congress Prints and Photographs Division; p. 41 © AP/Wide
World Photos

Library of Congress Cataloging-in-Publication Data

Somervill, Barbara A.
    The gold rush : buried treasure / Barbara A. Somervill.
    p. cm. — (Trailblazers of the West)
    Includes bibliographical references and index.
    ISBN 0-516-25129-5 (lib. bdg.) — ISBN 0-516-25099-X (pbk.)
    1. California—Gold discoveries—Juvenile literature. 2. California—History
1846–1850—Juvenile literature. 3. Frontier and pioneer life—California—
Juvenile literature. 4. Mining camps—California—History—19th century—
Juvenile literature. 5. Gold mines and mining—California—History—19th
century—Juvenile literature. I. Title. II. Series.

F865.S75 2005
979.4'03—dc22
                                                            2004021455

CONTENTS

INTRODUCTION

In 1848, boys selling newspapers across the country had an important headline to announce. "Extra! Extra!" they shouted. "Gold has been found in California!"

Americans wondered if this good news could be true. Soon enough, though, samples of the precious yellow metal were being passed around. The precious metal came in dust, flakes, and nuggets. When the governor of California sent President James K. Polk $3,900 worth of gold, the whole nation sat up and took notice.

Rumors of gold in California soon drifted through every American city. People spread stories about gold nuggets the size of grapes,

It was tales of gold such as this 9-ounce (280-gram) nugget that helped spread gold fever. Today, this much gold would be worth about $3,800.

and even melons. Some claimed that the gold was just lying on the ground. They said it was just waiting for people to come out and pick it up!

The dream of amazing wealth was too hard for many people to pass up. The discovery drew Americans from Maine to Mississippi. Blacksmiths lay down their hammers. Farmers walked away from their fields. Thousands of people left their jobs, homes, and families behind. In fact, people from all over the world set out for California, hoping to strike it rich.

The people who fled west to mine gold were called prospectors. Most of these people left for California in 1849. Because of this, they were called forty-niners. Many of these people went through a difficult journey. Many of them found their lives forever changed when they reached California. All of these new miners suffered from the same disease—gold fever.

Prospectors from all over America packed up their gear and headed for California in search of gold.

CHAPTER 1

CATCHING GOLD FEVER

January 24, 1848, was a quiet Monday morning. James Wilson Marshall walked along the creek near Sutter's Mill in California. Marshall's business partner, John Sutter, owned the mill. Sutter also ran a large farm with twelve thousand head of cattle and ten thousand sheep. His farm produced 40,000 bushels of wheat.

Marshall didn't know it at the time, but he was about to discover something that would turn a quiet town into the center of a nation's attention and change the history of America.

During his walk, Marshall looked into the shallow creek. What he saw shocked him. It was a shiny rock. Marshall pounded the object between two rocks. The object flattened but

James Wilson Marshall, the man who discovered the gold that started the gold rush, never struck it rich. He was unable to make a legal claim for the precious metal and his other businesses failed.

did not crumble. Excited, he brought the rock to Jenny Wimmer, the cook at the Sutter's Mill camp. Jenny dropped it into a cooking pot filled with a chemical called lye. If the rock dissolved, it could not be gold. However, the harsh chemicals did not damage Marshall's discovery. That's how Marshall knew that his piece of ore was gold.

Sutter and Marshall tried to keep the news about the discovery a secret. They didn't have much luck. Once word got out, the promise of becoming rich thrilled the hardworking men at the mills. In their free time, they began to look for gold in nearby streams. Henry Bigler, one of the part-time prospectors, wrote about the gold he found. He guessed in his diary that he found about one hundred dollars worth of gold every week. Bigler and others would leave their fellow workers when they had spare time. They would claim to be going on hunts for deer and ducks. Yet their hunt was really for gold.

The News Gets Around

Even the mill workers couldn't keep the news to themselves. They spread the word by writing to their friends. On March 15, 1848, the *Californian*, a San Francisco newspaper, broke the story. GOLD MINE FOUND, the paper reported. About three thousand men came from Oregon to see if they could find more of the precious metal. Still, most people did not believe the story was true.

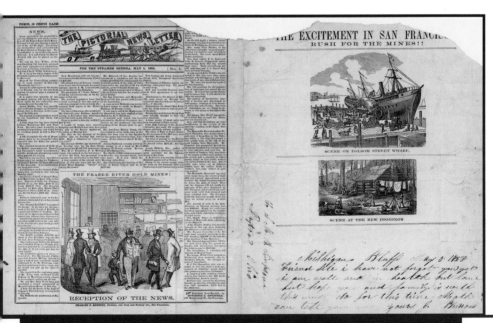

Newspapers everywhere carried stories of gold in California. This California newsletter reads, THE EXCITEMENT IN SAN FRANCISCO. RUSH FOR THE MINES!!

Word Spreads to Washington

In June 1848, California governor, R. B. Mason, toured the gold fields. After his tour, Mason guessed that about four thousand men were mining there! He believed that each day miners were uncovering between thirty and fifty thousand dollars worth of gold.

Mason collected ore samples and sent them to President James K. Polk in Washington, D.C. Mason wanted to prove to the president that there was gold at Sutter's Mill. In December 1848, President Polk announced that the rumors of gold in California were true.

The next day, reports about Polk's announcement appeared in newspapers everywhere. The *Hartford Daily Courant* reported: "Gold is picked up in pure lumps." The article said that many men, including soldiers and sailors, were quitting their jobs and heading out West.

Elephant Dreams

The forty-niners compared their experience to "seeing the elephant." This phrase came from an old tale of a farmer who heard that the circus was coming to town. At that time, circus parades usually featured elephants. The farmer had never seen an elephant and very much wanted to. He loaded his wagon with crops and went to the market in town. Upon seeing the circus parade, the farmer's horses panicked. The horses overturned the wagon and ruined the crops. But that didn't make any difference to the farmer. "I don't care," he said, "for I have seen the elephant." To the forty-niners, "seeing the elephant" represented both the troubles they might find on their journey to California, or like the farmer's seeing his elephant, a great experience.

Yet before they found any gold, the prospectors would have to get to California. In 1849, there was no quick or easy route. All routes cost money, took months, and could be dangerous. The forty-niners were about to find this out.

NORTH AMERICA

San Francisco

Independence

New York City

Atlantic Ocean

Panama

Pacific Ocean

SOUTH AMERICA

Cape Horn

KEY

Land Route

Combination

Water Route

CHAPTER 2

BY LAND AND SEA

Forty-niners used three ways to get to California. They could travel completely by land. They could travel by sea. Or they could use a combination of the two. Prospectors from the Midwest usually traveled by land. People from the East Coast often went by ship or by a combination of land and sea.

Wagon Ride

Overland routes began in Midwest cities such as St. Joseph and Independence, Missouri. There, the prospectors prepared to head to California on wagon trains. Before the trip could begin, each person needed to shop for supplies. Travelers had to stock up on tents,

In the mid-nineteenth century, prospectors flocked to California by land or sea, or a combination of the

guns, and wagons. They also had to purchase oxen and mules to carry their heavy loads. Shop owners grew rich off these prospectors heading across the Great Plains.

Of course, the forty-niners also had to buy food. Each person might buy 150 pounds (68 kilograms) of flour, 50 pounds (23 kg) of beans, 10 pounds (4.5 kg) each of sugar, bacon, and coffee. At the start of a trip, travelers feasted on fresh eggs and chicken. By the journey's end, meals were usually much simpler. Bacon, beans, and biscuits were often eaten three times a day.

Trial of the Trail

Journeys west began in mid-spring. If travelers left for their destinations too early, there would be no grass for their livestock to feed on. If they left too late, they might be trapped by blizzards before reaching California.

Oxen and mules were strong animals, but there was a limit to the amount of weight even they could pull. To lighten their animals' loads, people often had to walk to California beside their wagons! Still, some like Harriet Ward

In this painting, a wagon train of forty-niners marches through mountains in Oregon on its way to California.

enjoyed the adventure. "I had so often read and heard of the difficulties and dangers of the overland route to California," Ward wrote in her diary in 1853. "I find from experience that the pleasure thus far quite overbalances it."

Other travelers found the journey exhausting. Diseases were a common hazard of overland travel. In those days, cholera killed many people on wagon trains. This disease causes vomiting and diarrhea. Without treatment, severe cholera can kill within hours.

Many prospectors believed that Native Americans presented another threat. However, in the early days of the gold rush, Native Americans traded with the forty-niners.

Death Valley was a harsh desert that claimed the lives of many who dared to cross it.

They bought thread, cloth, pots, and guns from them. In turn, the forty-niners received fresh bison meat, fish, and antelope.

After weeks of walking, wagon trains reached the South Pass through the Rocky Mountains. They had traveled nearly 900 miles (1,450 kilometers) from Missouri. By this time, people, oxen, and mules were very weary. To lighten loads, dishes, books, and other luxuries were dumped on the trail.

Once the forty-niners made it through the Rockies, another obstacle was waiting: the desert. Some wagon trains took a southern route that crossed through Death Valley. Travelers needed plenty of food and water to make the trip. Death Valley's springs did not offer much drinkable water, and many people died of thirst. Wagons often passed the bones, skulls, and other remains of dead people who had died trying to cross the desert.

Other wagon trains chose a northern route. There, forty-niners passed through the high desert. Still, temperatures sizzled by day and dropped to near freezing at night. Rattlesnakes and scorpions were a constant source of danger for travelers.

Finally, the prospectors reached the Sierras. This mountain chain was their last barrier to California. Sierra trails proved dangerous. Mules often lost their footing and fell down mountainsides, taking the wagons with them. Men and women often struggled to hold wagons back from racing down steep slopes. People were often killed or injured by runaway wagons.

Braving the Waves

The sea route covered 13,000 miles (20,800 km) or more from East Coast ports such as New York or Baltimore to San Francisco, California. The trip took four to eight months. Sea travelers did not face endless miles of walking, snakes, or dangerous mountain trails. Instead, they had to deal with boredom, horrible food, and hurricanes.

Excited passengers fared well at first. However, gold fever soon gave way to seasickness. Gales and hurricanes tossed the ships around. Shipboard meals were often nothing more than rotten beef. Passengers also ate hard flour biscuits called hardtack. The freshest meat on board the ship was often living inside these biscuits: beetlelike bugs called weevils! People pounded their hardtack on a table to shake the weevils out. Mostly, they just ate them because that was easier than trying to remove the weevils from the hardtack.

FRONTIER FACT

The seawater at Cape Horn was so cold that a person falling overboard died within a couple of minutes!

Ships such as the steamer Hartford *set out on the long journey from New York to California in the late 1840s.*

Then came the brutal weather of Cape Horn. Cape Horn is located at the southern tip of South America. Ships there battled storms with winds of 100 miles (160 km) per hour. Passengers huddled in cabins and sometimes tied themselves onto their beds. This prevented them from being bounced around their cabins when the seas got rough. Yet even after making it past the cape, weary travelers had at least two months of travel ahead of them. Ships still had to sail up the western coasts of South America, Central America, and the United States. Finally, the ships anchored in San Francisco harbor. Passengers were happy to finally stand on dry land again.

Many forty-niners traveled the route that took them over sea and land. For them, crossing the Panama jungles (above) meant experiencing all kinds of wonders and dangers.

Welcome to the Jungle

The third type of journey included travel by both land and sea. It took forty-niners through the Caribbean Sea to Panama. There, they headed overland to the Pacific Ocean. This trip was the most expensive of the three.

Crossing Panama provided beautiful views of the jungle. On their journey, huge lilies, palm trees, and colorful butterflies dazzled forty-niners. It was a side of nature most of them had never seen before.

The jungle also had its share of dangers. Many travelers came down with malaria, a disease that causes chills and high fever. Yellow fever also killed many forty-niners. Both deadly viruses were spread by mosquitoes. Poisonous snakes slithered through the jungle. Insects became a constant annoyance.

Natives armed with huge cane knives charged large sums of money to guide travelers the 60 miles (96 km) across the land. The guides provided a pay-or-else service: either pay the fee or deal with an angry native with a huge knife! But once on the Pacific Coast side of Panama, the forty-niners were not always joyous. In fact, they discovered that very few ships came to take them to San Francisco. Travelers waited days—even months—before they were picked up.

No Time to Rest

Once prospectors reached San Francisco, they were relieved but weary. Remarkably, their travels still hadn't ended. To get to the gold fields from San Francisco, they now had to travel up the Sacramento River in smaller vessels. Sailing up the Sacramento River cost anywhere from five to fifty dollars. The forty-niners paid whatever boat owners demanded. They had no choice.

CHAPTER 3

LIFE IN A MINING CAMP

Once prospectors reached California, they needed a grubstake. A grubstake was an amount of food and supplies loaned to miners by local business owners and residents. Forty-niners received supplies such as mining tools, a tent, warm clothes, and a weapon. In exchange, the miners would pay back an agreed-upon amount of any gold they found.

Prospectors faced another big challenge. Most of them did not know where to find gold. They had heard of gold strikes in places such as Yankee Jim's, French Corral, or Coyote Diggings. Yet they often had no idea where these places were. Maps were often incorrect or misleading. Sometimes, three or

In this photo, teams of eager forty-niners ride their loaded wagons on their journeys toward striking it rich.

four different camps were given the same name. Of course, none of the maps told prospectors exactly where to *dig*!

Still, anxious miners headed into the hills. Word of any major strikes spread faster than wildfire. Within weeks, a one-tent camp blossomed into a small city. From there, towns emerged, with banks, saloons, and other businesses to take care of the growing population.

Mining camps weren't very comfortable. Some people built hotels for prospectors. While they went up quickly, these hotels weren't built well. The walls and ceilings weren't made of wood or concrete. Instead, they were made of cloth and canvas. Getting a good night's sleep was nearly impossible. Sleeping prospectors would often wake up to the sound of people talking from several rooms away!

Going for the Gold

Once forty-niners spotted gold, they had to separate it from the earth. The tool that helped them separate ore from dirt was often a simple wash pan made of tin or iron.

Wash pans had flat bottoms, much like pie plates. While standing or sitting in a stream, miners would scoop up dirt in their wash pans from the bottom of the stream. They swished the water and dirt around. Any pieces of gold would settle to the bottom of the pan. The pans worked because the gold was heavier than the rocks and water.

However, the miners quickly grew tired of having to squat in ice-cold water for hours panning for gold.

Prospectors used tin wash pans to separate gold from dirt and rocks.

To solve this problem, miners designed a few other items to help them get their gold a little faster. A rocker, or sluice, was one of their inventions. Sluices came in several different styles. They were boxes, usually made of wood. The bottom of these boxes were lined with wood rails called riffles. As dirt, rock, and water sifted through the sluice, heavy pieces of gold collected behind the riffles. Waste dirt and rock washed away.

Digging for gold was a straightforward process. However, it took forty-niners hours of backbreaking work just to yield a few ounces of gold. In good weather, miners dug, panned, sifted, and washed from dawn until dusk. They pocketed every piece of gold they found and headed back to camp. Sore and exhausted, they fell asleep. Then they started the whole process over again, early the next morning.

Shantytowns

A single gold strike drew hundreds of miners. Tents and shanties went up, and a town formed almost instantly. Once towns began to grow, bankers arrived and built the town's first bank.

In this photograph, forty-niners stand by their sluice, or rocker.

Miners could deposit their gold in the banks. The banks kept gold treasures safe from theft.

Every mining town had a general store to sell supplies. Store owners often charged ten times what items normally cost. Prices soared as mining camps grew. Eggs could cost up to three dollars each. Today, that would be about sixty-one dollars! An onion could cost two dollars. A needle and thread could have a price tag of almost eight dollars.

Towns such as Bodie, California, popped up during the gold rush in the 1850s. Bodie became a town full of miners, gamblers, robbers, and gunfighters. It was known as the roughest town in the West.

Miners paid in gold. A pinch of dust equaled one dollar. An ounce was worth sixteen dollars. A small glass filled with gold dust bought one hundred dollars in goods. A large glass held one thousand dollars' worth. Payment was sloppy. Many miners paid in gold, accidentally spilling as much gold dust on the floorboards as they put on the shop's counter!

Over time, professionals moved into the town. These people provided the miners with needed services. Blacksmiths fixed axes and picks or made new tools. Doctors, dentists, and lawyers also found work in the mining camps. Quickly, a place that people came to hoping to strike it rich became a place to call home.

Crime and Punishment

Newcomers had to live by the laws each town made, or suffer the consequences. Most towns had crime of some type, such as fighting. Fistfights sometimes began as entertainment, only to end in terrible violence. Claim-jumping, the act of stealing someone's legal mining area, also occurred. Guilty claim-jumpers were often forced out of town. Another crime that sometimes occurred was theft. During the day, miners left their belongings in their tents. This made it easy for others to steal their goods.

FRONTIER FACT

Surprisingly, theft was rare. That's probably because the crime would be punished by beating or hanging the guilty person.

Working Women

For women, mining towns offered greater opportunity than anywhere in the United States. Men paid happily for a home-cooked meal. One miner's wife reported that a woman with cooking skills could earn sixteen dollars per week for every man she cooked for. Women in mining towns whipped up fresh-baked bread, stews, and roasts. Forty-niners would gladly pay for all of it. One woman sold eighteen thousand dollars' worth of fruit pies in one year!

Cooking wasn't the only job for women in mining towns. Women received pay for sewing and ironing. A woman who washed clothes could make as much as one hundred dollars a week. Compared to women's regular wages, this was a fortune. In the late 1840s, for example, a female worker at Lowell mills in Massachusetts earned under two dollars per week. Schoolteachers received only about two hundred dollars a year.

Black Prospectors

During the days of the gold rush, slavery was legal in many parts of the United States. Black slaves worked for slaveholders who owned businesses such as farms or plantations. Many slave owners brought their slaves to California to do the heavy work of panning and digging.

In this photo, a black prospector works in Auburn Ravine, California, in 1852.

Some slaves earned their freedom by working in the gold fields in this way. Free blacks also played a role in the rush for riches. By 1850, thousands of freemen worked the fields of California. It is believed that in 1850 the wealthiest black area in the United States was in California.

This engraving from the 1850s shows Chinese miners at their mining camp.

From Foreign Shores

Foreigners flooded San Francisco's streets during the gold rush. They came from all corners of the globe, including Mexico, Chile, and China. Not all foreigners received a hearty welcome. The Chinese, in particular, were outcasts among the miners. Some miners resented anyone mining American gold that was not American. Those miners forgot that their grandparents or great-grandparents had come from another country, too.

Most Chinese hoped to get rich and return to China. They lived together in groups called Chinatowns. Those living in Chinatowns kept their distance from the other miners. They ate Chinese food, wore Chinese clothing, and kept Chinese customs. They did not learn to speak English. They lived and worked separately from the other miners. Still, the Chinese and other foreign-born people enriched California. They brought new foods, customs, and cultures. The changes helped make the state unique and exciting.

CHAPTER 4

THE LEGACY OF GOLD

By 1853, nearly 100,000 prospectors were
working the gold fields. They mined about
sixty-seven million dollars of gold. However, the
gold rush was already winding down. The gold
available by panning or sluicing had run out.
Prospectors couldn't use tin pans to find the
little gold that was left. Mining the rest of the
gold would require heavy digging equipment.
Within a year, miners would leave the fields and
head home.

California Grows Up

The major part of the gold rush lasted for six
years. Yet its effects lasted far longer. No one
could have imagined how much California
would change because of the gold rush.

*By 1854, heavy mining equipment replaced panning
and sluicing. This is when the prospectors packed it
up and went home.*

This print from around 1851 shows a scene of the San Francisco area. The promise of gold was one of the main reasons for the city's rapid growth and development.

Before gold was discovered, only about five hundred people moved that far west each year. In 1849, more than twenty-five thousand people arrived in California. That's about five hundred people *each week*!

California had become a U.S. territory in 1848. Only fourteen thousand people lived there at the time. Within two years, the population was over ninety-two thousand. The territory now had enough people to become a state. The state's population continued to climb. Today, California is the most heavily populated state in the United States. It is also the state with the most new arrivals each year.

Because of the gold rush, new cities started. San Francisco grew from a small harbor town to a bustling urban center. John Sutter's son founded the city that became the state capital, Sacramento. Most mining towns disappeared when the gold ran out, but some became cities. Marysville and Placerville are two cities that still exist today.

Winners and Losers

Many people lost money during the gold rush. Surprisingly, the failures included James Marshall and John Sutter. James Marshall, who found the first gold nugget, was penniless by 1872. In that year, the California state legislature agreed to give Marshall a small pension in honor of his important role in state history. But by 1878, the state stopped giving him the pension.

John Sutter made money selling food and grain. A poor businessman, Sutter ran up debts. He managed his ranch badly. He went bankrupt. Sutter also asked for government help. However, he received none and he died a poor man.

A few miners became rich after finding massive amounts of gold. John Sullivan, an ox-team driver, used his twenty-six thousand dollars of gold to start a bank. John Bidwell, a wagon train guide, made one of the richest gold strikes. Using his fortune, Bidwell built a ranch on 20,000 acres (8,094 hectares) of land.

The gold rush led to the building of towns and cities. It drew immigrants who added new culture and customs to a growing nation. Business, banking, and transportation prospered because of the gold rush. Yet behind these developments was the hard work and pioneer spirit of men and women who took great risks to make their lives better. The memory of these trailblazers of the West are the true legacy of the great California gold rush.

FRONTIER FACT

John Bidwell eventually went into politics. In 1892, he ran for president of the United States. He lost the election to Grover Cleveland.

STRIKING IT RICH WITHOUT GOLD

Levi Strauss

Businesses that set up shop in California often outlasted the mining camps. Two famous gold rush successes were Levi Strauss and Philip Armour. Strauss headed for San Francisco in 1850 with some canvas tent material. He used this canvas to make heavy pants for miners. Strauss sold the pants as fast as he could make them. By 1900, Strauss's denim pants, with their copper rivets, were famous. Levi's jeans are wildly popular, even today.

Philip Armour began his career digging ditches in California's gold fields. With the money he earned, Armour opened a meat market in Placerville. Armour moved his meat business to Milwaukee when the gold rush ended. Today, his Armour Star products—from hot dogs to roast beef to chili—are big sellers throughout the nation.

NEW WORDS

bankrupt (bangk-ruhpt) when people or companies cannot pay their debts

cholera (kol-ur-uh) a dangerous disease that causes severe sickness and diarrhea

gale (gale) a very strong wind

grubstake (gruhb-stayk) a quantity of food and other supplies needed by prospectors before setting out

hardtack (hard-tak) a type of hard, prebaked biscuit

immigrant (im-uh-gruhnt) a person who moves from one country to another

lye (lye) a strong cleaning agent

malaria (muh-lair-ee-uh) a disease that gives people high fevers and chills

nugget (nuhg-it) a chunk of metal ore

ore (or) a rock that contains metal

outcast (**out**-kast) someone who is not accepted by other people

pension (**pen**-shuhn) an amount of money paid regularly to someone who has retired from work

prospector (**pross**-pekt-or) a person who looks for gold or other minerals

resent (ri-**zent**) to feel hurt or angry about something that has been done or said to you

rivet (**riv**-it) a strong metal bolt used to fasten things together

shanty (**shan**-tee) a crudely built shelter or hut

weevil (**wee**-vuhl) a beetlelike bug

yellow fever (**yel**-oh **fee**-vur) a disease caused by a virus spread by mosquitoes

yield (**yeeld**) to produce something

FOR FURTHER READING

Goldsmith, Connie. *Lost in Death Valley: The True Story of Four Families in California's Gold Rush.* Brookfield, CT: Twenty-First Century Books, Inc., 2001.

Gregory, Kristiana. *Seeds of Hope: The Gold Rush Diary of Susanna Fairchild, 1849.* New York: Scholastic, Inc., 2003.

Ito, Tom. *The California Gold Rush.* San Diego, CA: Lucent Books, 1998.

Saffer, Barbara. *The California Gold Rush.* Broomall, PA: Mason Crest Publishers, 2002.

Schroeder, Lisa Golden. *California Gold Rush Cooking.* Minneapolis, MN: Capstone Press, 2001.

ORGANIZATIONS

The California Historical Society
678 Mission Street
San Francisco, CA 94105
(415) 357-1848
www.californiahistoricalsociety.org

The Society of California Pioneers
300 Fourth Street
San Francisco, CA 94107
(415) 957-1849
www.californiapioneers.org

WEB SITES

Discovery of Gold by John A. Sutter
www.sfmuseum.org/hist2/gold.html
This link is part of the Museum of San Francisco's
Web site. The museum's online exhibit about the
gold rush includes entries from John Sutter's
diary, images of forty-niners at work, time lines,
and much more.

Gold Rush! California's Untold Stories
www.museumca.org/goldrush/index.html
Want to learn more about gold fever, immigrant
forty-niners, and the art of the gold rush? This
Web site from the Oakland Museum of California
has all this and more.

Women in the Gold Rush
www.goldrush.com/~joann/
Learn about the lives and experiences of women
during the gold rush era.

INDEX

B
bankrupt, 39
Bidwell, John, 40

C
California, 5–6, 9,
    11–13, 15–17, 19–20,
    25, 32–33, 35, 37–40
Cape Horn, 21
cholera, 17

D
Death Valley, 19

F
forty-niners, 6, 13,
    15–19, 22–23, 25–26,
    28, 32

G
gale, 20
grubstake, 25

H
hardtack, 20

I
immigrants, 40

L
lye, 10

M
malaria, 22
Marshall, James Wilson,
    9–10, 39
Mason, R. B., 12
mining camp, 26,
    29–30, 39

N
Native Americans, 17
nugget, 5, 39

O
ore, 10, 12, 26

P
Panama, 22–23
pension, 39
Polk, James K., 5, 12
prospector, 6, 10, 13,
    15–16, 19, 23,
    25–26, 32, 37

R
riffle, 28

INDEX

ABOUT THE AUTHOR

Barbara A. Somervill is a lifelong learner. She writes books for children, video scripts, magazine articles, and textbooks. She is an avid reader and traveler and enjoys movies and live theater. She was raised in New York. She's also lived in Canada, Australia, California, and South Carolina.